AF131438

BOOK ANALYSIS

Written by Eli Cumings

Measure for Measure

by William Shakespeare

WILLIAM SHAKESPEARE

ENGLISH PLAYWRIGHT AND POET

- **Born in Stratford-upon-Avon in 1564.**
- **Died in Stratford-upon-Avon in 1616.**
- **Notable works:**
  - *Venus and Adonis* (1593), poem
  - *Hamlet* (1603), play
  - *Macbeth* (1623), play

William Shakespeare is regarded as the most influential writer in English history. His 37 plays have been performed countless times, and have been reproduced and adapted across a broad range of periods and cultural contexts. As well as the plays, which can be loosely divided into tragedies, histories and comedies, Shakespeare wrote a number of narrative poems and sonnets. He also had an indelible influence on the English language itself, bringing a huge variety of words and phrases – as varied as "swagger", "bubble", "mind's eye" and "heart of gold" – into regular usage.

Shakespeare married Anne Hathaway in 1582 and had three children with her. Their only son, Hamnet, died at the age of 11. Very little else is known about Shakespeare's life, which he spent between Stratford-upon-Avon and London. It is clear, however, that his literary talents were matched by a shrewd entrepreneurial spirit. He made a number of profitable investments in his lifetime, which gave him the financial freedom to devote himself to acting and writing. In 1599, Shakespeare and his acting company (The Lord Chamberlain's Men) built the Globe Theatre on the banks of the River Thames in London. Many of Shakespeare's greatest plays were written to be performed at this theatre.

MEASURE FOR MEASURE

A 'PROBLEM' PLAY

- **Genre:** play
- **Reference edition:** Shakespeare, W. (2008) *Measure for Measure*. London: Norton.
- **1ˢᵗ edition:** 1623
- **Themes:** justice, sin, lust, mercy, deception

Measure for Measure was first performed in 1604 and is presumed to have been written shortly before this. Its most important source is *Promos and Cassandra* (1578), an unperformed play by George Whetstone (English dramatist, 1544-1587). In the earlier play, a corrupt judge forces a young woman to yield up her virginity in exchange for her brother's life. In Shakespeare's play, the heroine manages – with the help of a willing replacement – to avoid submitting to the antagonist's request. However, the play still confronts the issues of corruption, disempowerment and coercion. The prominence of these weighty issues, along with the play's dark tone and troubling ending, means that *Measure for Measure* is often given the designation of a 'problem play'.

SUMMARY

ANGELO LAYS DOWN THE LAW

The Duke of Vienna informs Escalus, an old lord, that he will be leaving the city for a while. He appoints the well-respected Angelo to rule in his stead, passing all of his legal powers over the city and citizens to him. After pretending to leave the city, the Duke approaches a Friar for assistance. He reveals that he is concerned about the depravity demonstrated by his people, but is reluctant to enforce the city's harsh laws. By putting the morally upright Angelo in charge, he will be able to observe the effects of stricter systems of justice. He intends to return to the city in disguise to watch the situation unfold and asks the Friar to equip him with robes for this purpose.

In the streets of Vienna, the raucous Lucio banters with two gentlemen, each accusing the other of having a host of sexually transmitted diseases. During their sparring match, Mistress Overdone – the Madam of a brothel which the three men have frequented – appears and tells them that a young gentleman named Claudio is being taken to prison for the crime of fornication. The evidence against him is that his lover, Juliet, is pregnant. As the men depart to find out more about Claudio's plight, Pompey the clown reveals that all the brothels in the suburbs are to be closed on Angelo's command – further evidence of his quest against iniquity.

Lucio comes across Claudio and Juliet being led to jail by the Provost, or jailor. When he is questioned about the cause of his arrest, Claudio blames human nature, saying that all are disposed towards bodily sin but acting upon this necessitates punishment. However, Claudio also reveals a fact which would have absolved him in the eyes of many audience members: he and Juliet had promised themselves to one another in private – a fact which, along with the consummation, carried the same weight as an official ceremony in common law. Despite this, Angelo has elected to enforce the death penalty against Claudio in order to set a precedent. Having tried and failed to contact the Duke to beg for mercy, Claudio asks Lucio to send a message to his sister asking her to speak with Angelo on his behalf.

AN ULTIMATUM IS PRESENTED

Lucio seeks out Claudio's sister Isabella in the convent, where she is soon to take her vows as a nun. After he has informed her of her brother's plight, she travels to the courts of justice where she pleads with Angelo for mercy. Over the course of her pleading, she asks Angelo to look within himself to ensure he is not guilty of any similar fault. In the end, he agrees to think about what she has said and asks her to return the following day for an answer. In a soliloquy, he reveals that he is attracted to her on account of her many virtues.

The following day, Angelo appears in a state of agitation. He has attempted to pray, but can only think of Isabella. When she returns for an answer, he presents her with an ultimatum: either she surrenders her body to his lusts, or her brother dies. Isabella rejects him and threatens to tell the world of his iniquity. However, Angelo informs her that her accusations will not be believed. He transforms his ultimatum into a threat: if she does not submit, he will ensure that Claudio's death is long and torturous. Isabella laments the trap which Angelo has set for her, but is convinced that Claudio would rather sacrifice himself than his sister's virtue.

Back at the prison, the disguised Duke counsels Claudio to prepare himself for death. Soon afterwards, Isabella arrives to speak to her brother, and the Duke and Provost conceal themselves to eavesdrop. When Isabella sets out Angelo's proposition, Claudio initially rejects it: "Thou shalt not do't" (3.1.102). However, as their conversation progresses and he begins to voice his crippling fear of death, he becomes more open to the suggestion and eventually begs his sister to save him. She responds with horror and entirely rejects the possibility. At this point the Duke comes out of hiding and reveals that he has overheard their conversation.

THE 'FRIAR' OFFERS A SOLUTION

At present, the disguised Duke observes, Isabella has no evidence that Angelo has committed a misdeed: it could be that he is merely testing her. In order for his sins to be fully exposed, they must encourage him to follow through on his suggestions. The Duke explains that Angelo was previously engaged to a woman named Mariana, whom he forsook when her brother was lost at sea, along with her dowry. Despite his poor treatment of her, Mariana still loves him. Therefore, the Duke advises Isabella to accept Angelo's proposal but send Mariana in her stead. Once this liaison comes to light, Angelo will be forced to marry her.

Isabella and the Duke visit Mariana to explain the plan and she agrees to take part. The Duke points out that the union between Angelo and Mariana will not be sinful, as their spoken agreement – like that of Claudio and Juliet – constitutes a "pre-contract" to marriage (4.1.68). After Isabella has arranged the tryst with Angelo, the Duke returns to the prison, where he expects a pardon to arrive for Claudio. Instead, a messenger appears with an instruction to execute Claudio as planned. In addition to this, Angelo requests that Claudio's head be presented to him as confirmation that the execution has taken place.

The Duke, still disguised, asks the Provost to delay Claudio's death to give him time to uncover Angelo's misdeeds. In order to facilitate this, he suggests that the Provost appease Angelo by sending him the head of another prisoner – the murderer Barnadine. The Provost and executioner attempt to execute Barnadine, but he flatly refuses on the grounds that he has been drinking all night: "I will not consent to die this day, that's certain" (4.3.48-49). When Barnadine returns to his cell, the Provost reveals that another prisoner, a pirate named Ragusine who conveniently resembles Claudio, has just died. They send his head to Angelo.

DUKE VINCENTIO RETURNS

Angelo and Escalus receive letters informing them that the Duke is returning to the city. Angelo is fearful, but reasons that Isabella will not speak up against him as the news of their liaison would tarnish her reputation. He also believes that the weight of his own reputation will dissuade her. The Duke arrives at the city gates in his normal attire and greets Angelo and Escalus. As they walk into the city, Isabella kneels before the Duke and begs him for justice. She outlines Angelo's crimes and the Duke listens intently. In the end, however, he dismisses her story as malicious slander and orders that she be taken to prison. He also orders that the Friar be brought forth, declaring that he is the engineer of the scheme against Angelo.

Once the Duke has returned to court, Mariana enters in a veil and reveals her part in the story. Angelo admits that he was once engaged to her, but denies that he has seen or heard from her since. Once again, he accuses the Friar of inciting the women to deception and asks permission to punish them all for the conspiracy. The Duke grants him permission to do so and departs. Shortly afterwards, he returns in disguise as the Friar. Despite his attempts to defend himself and the women, Escalus orders that he be taken to prison. Before this can happen, however, Lucio pulls off his hood and reveals the Duke.

When Angelo realises his treachery is apparent, he confesses to his crimes and requests death as punishment. Instead, the Duke orders him to marry Mariana and sends them off to complete the ceremony. The Duke then turns to Isabella and apologises for her brother's death, saying that it occurred too quickly for him to avert. When Angelo and Mariana return from the ceremony, the Duke sentences him to death; the marriage was intended to pardon her morally and to give her legal rights to Angelo's wealth. Upon hearing this, Mariana falls to her knees to beg Isabella for mercy. Though still convinced that her brother is dead, Isabella yields and successfully asks the Duke to spare Angelo. In the play's closing moments, Claudio returns from prison alive and well and is instructed to marry Juliet. The Duke also proposes to Isabella, who responds only with silence.

CHARACTER STUDY

THE DUKE

Vincentio, the Duke of Vienna, is a highly ambivalent character. At the outset of the play, he reveals his quandary: his lax approach to justice has allowed the city to become lawless, but he is reluctant to enforce the strict rules which have been unenforced for 14 years. His decision to leave the city and put the harsher Angelo in charge could, then, be read as an abandonment of his responsibilities. However, he does not trust Angelo entirely and returns to the city in disguise to keep an eye on him. Indeed, it may be that the entire scheme is a ploy to uncover Angelo's true nature. After explaining his plan to the friar, the Duke observes: "Hence shall we see / If power change purpose, what our seemers be" (1.4.53-54).

Later in the play, the Duke has a number of opportunities to alleviate the other characters' suffering, but chooses to save all happy revelations until the last possible minute. This tendency can, to some extent, be explained by a desire to draw out the limits of Angelo's iniquity and Isabella's goodness. From another perspective, however, his decisions to conceal Claudio's survival from his sister and to delay the revelation of his identity as the Friar seem senseless and even callous. Furthermore, his decision to marry Isabella at the end of the play demonstrates a failure to understand her desires or recognise her choices. Some critics have therefore suggested that, in this respect, he is as bad as Angelo.

ANGELO

The interim leader appointed by the Duke enjoys a reputation as a strict and puritanical man. As expected, he immediately enforces the strictest of laws against promiscuity and fornication. Though he does not deny having been tempted in the past, he insists that he has never succumbed to such temptation. On these grounds, he is unafraid to enforce a harsh punishment against Claudio and insists that he should be held to the same standard if he ever falls. Though numerous of the play's characters appeal to his sense of mercy, he does not budge.

Whilst he is eventually tempted by Isabella's virtues, he claims to have been immune to all other women's charms: "Ever till now / When men were fond, I smiled and wondered how" (2.3.190-191). On this basis, it can be assumed that his engagement to Mariana was motivated by an opportunistic interest in her substantial dowry. This fact, along with his gross mistreatment of her once her dowry is lost, demonstrates some long-standing moral flaws in his character. The Duke's familiarity with this story raises further questions about his motivation for installing Angelo as interim leader.

ISABELLA

Isabella is incredibly pious and, initially, somewhat restrained in her speech. Her appeal to Angelo for mercy requires much encouragement and instruction from Lucio, who encourages her to use all the feminine charms available to her. She is entirely virtuous, preferring to die rather than give up her virginity. This assessment of the relative value of body and soul also applies to her brother: "Better it were a brother died at once / Than that a sister, by redeeming him, / Should die for ever" (2.4.107-109). The intensity of Isabella's religious convictions, a feature so central to the plot of *Measure of Measure*, is an invention of Shakespeare's; the sister in *Promos and Cassandra* does not aspire to be a nun, but does eventually relent and sleep with the deputy. Shakespeare's decision to make Isabella a devoted Catholic raises questions about the relative value of life and afterlife, body and soul. These questions are further compounded at the end of the play when the Duke, in spite of Isabella's intention to become a nun, decides to marry her. Her silence in response to his proposal has been the subject of a wide variety of interpretations by generations of directors and critics. Whilst the most optimistic have interpreted it as a sign of her refusal, the less hopeful have read it as horrified resignation.

CLAUDIO

Isabella's brother Claudio is a young man condemned for the crime of fornication. However, it is worth remembering that he and Juliet did not commit a straightforward crime. Private, legally-binding ceremonies of the kind they claim to have performed were often held in advance of public weddings in the early modern period. It is notable that Shakespeare's own first child, Susanna, was born five months after he and his wife Anne's public wedding ceremony.

Claudio, however, does not make any great efforts to defend himself in *Measure for Measure*. He is cynical about human nature, comparing lust to an insatiable desire for poison. His resignation adds to the drama of the situation, putting the onus entirely on Isabella to find a solution for his plight. Whilst he is initially philosophical about his execution, his increasingly horror at the reality of death leads him to beg his sister to agree to Angelo's request. Whilst Claudio's descent from resignation to desperate pleading could be played for laughs, his fear of mortality is too profound and relatable to be dismissed as pure comedy.

LUCIO

The raucous gentleman Lucio is one of the only characters who takes a positive view of sex, declaring that if he were the judge assigned to Claudio's case he would congratulate him. When he describes the supposed crime to Isabella, he uses rich harvest imagery which normalises sex and conception by linking it to natural seasonal processes (1.4.40-43). However, his persistent focus on sexually transmitted diseases somewhat undermines this sex-positive view. Lucio is also the source of surprisingly poignant advice. Counselling Isabella to go to her brother's aid, for example, he advises her "Our doubts are traitors, / And makes us lose the good we oft might win, / By fearing to attempt" (1.4.77-79). He also advises her throughout her conversation with Angelo, praising her arguments and suggesting amendments to her performance. Lucio however, is no hero. He abandons the mother of his child and, when he is forced to marry her, describes it as a fate worse than death. He also spreads malicious rumours which range from (relatively) harmless accusations of disease to treasonous accusations against the Duke.

ANALYSIS

A 'PROBLEM' PLAY

Measure for Measure has the basic hallmarks of a Shakespearean comedy: it represents the triumph of young lovers against adversity; makes use of disguises and deceptions; is filled with bawdy humour and wordplay; and ends with the promise of nuptials. However, the play stretches the limits of the comic genre with its difficult subject matter and ambivalent tone, and for this reason it is often described as a 'problem' comedy.

One of the play's tonal issues is its obsessive interest with death. At various points, Isabella represents death as a preferable alternative to dishonour and sin. This is an attitude common in Shakespearean tragedies, including *Othello* (1622), *Hamlet* (1603) and *Julius Caesar* (1623), in which characters would rather die than live on with an impaired reputation. Elsewhere in the play, however, this noble representation of death as a preferable option is entirely undermined. Claudio, for example, declares:

> "The weariest and most loathéd worldly life
> That age, ache, penury, and imprisonment
> Can lay on nature is a paradise
> To what we fear of death." (3.1.129-132)

For Claudio, even a wretched life is preferable to the unknown horrors of death. This grim perspective stands in stark contrast to the play's comic tone.

The ending of the play also stretches the limits of comic resolution. Though four marriages are proposed, the majority of these are highly unsettling: Angelo has requested death; Lucio claims that he would prefer death; and Isabella, who was on the verge of taking a nun's vows at the outset of the play, has made it clear that she would rather die than yield up her body. Whilst it is hard to imagine any audience interpreting this resolution as straightforwardly positive, the prevailing religious sensibilities of Shakespeare's contemporaries may have made a slight difference. Unlike Catholics, who perceived chastity as the most perfect state, Shakespeare's Protestant contemporaries rated productive marriage more highly. It is useful to bear this context in mind when reading the ending of *Measure for Measure*.

HUMAN NATURE

As he is led to prison by the Provost, Claudio observes: "Our natures do pursue, / Like rats that raven down their proper bane, / A thirsty evil; and when we drink we die" (1.2.108-110). Claudio describes sexual desire as a damaging force which has the potential to wreck the body like a 'bane', or poison. Despite its detrimental properties, this form of desire is considered as irresistible as the need to nourish oneself. Throughout the play, physical compulsions are shown to prevail over abstract social responsibilities, particularly when the laws which govern these behaviours are seen to be dormant.

Echoing Claudio's belief in humanity's susceptibility to evil, Isabella draws attention to mankind's 'natural guiltiness' when warning Angelo against hypocrisy:

> "Go to your bosom;
> Knock there, and ask your heart what it doth know
> That's like my brother's fault. If it confess
> A natural guiltiness, such as is his,
> Let it not sound a thought upon your tongue
> Against my brother's life." (2.2.139-144)

Isabella argues that Angelo should not prosecute Claudio for his crimes unless he is entirely certain that he is not liable to succumb to the same fault. This argument is based on the assumption that all men possess some degree of 'natural guiltiness'. This assumption is reminiscent of the notion of original sin: the idea that all humans are predisposed to evil, as they have inherited the sin of Adam and Eve.

According to public opinion, Angelo is entirely without this 'natural guiltiness'. When discussing his appointment, the Duke remarks: "Lord Angelo is precise [...] scarce confesses / That his blood flows" (1.3.50-52). Likewise, Lucio describes Angelo as: "a man whose blood / Is very snow-broth; one who never feels / the wanton stings and motions of the sense" (1.4.56-58). Angelo is initially described as a frosty superhuman who is not liable to the kinds of bodily urges which Claudio and Isabella describe. However, the play reveals that he is very much susceptible to temptation. All humans – or, more specifically, all *men* – are susceptible to bodily lust. This conclusion paints a damning picture of human nature.

JUSTICE: HUMAN AND DIVINE

The title of the play, which is taken from Matthew 7:2, indicates its concern with justice. Out of context, the quotation seems to encourage the 'eye for an eye' mode of justice which is common in Shakespearean tragedies. This sense of equivalence and proportionality is particularly appropriate for a play where individual humans are repeatedly substituted for one another: Mariana for Isabella in the 'bed trick'; Ragusine for Claudio in the 'head trick'.

The full Biblical quotation, however, reads:

> "Judge not, that ye be not judged.
> For with what judgment ye judge, ye shall be judged: and with what measure ye mete, it shall be measured to you again."
> Matthew 7:1-2

The scripture is a warning *against* the reciprocal 'eye for an eye' form of justice. Instead, it encourages individuals to look within themselves and refrain from judging others for crimes they are also guilty of. Given the 'natural guiltiness' to which all men are disposed, it is fitting that mercy rather than judgement should rule.

The question of who is entitled to enforce justice is addressed repeatedly in the play. During her initial audience with Angelo, Isabella points out that all humans were forsaken until Jesus died for their sins. Justice, she argues, should be a heavenly rather than an earthly enterprise. This argument is further strengthened by the inconsistency of earthly laws: is it appropriate to execute Claudio for an act which, according to many, is not even a crime?

FURTHER REFLECTION

SOME QUESTIONS TO THINK ABOUT...

- Why does the Duke choose to leave the city in Angelo's hands?
- Characters like Lucio often use sexually trans-mitted diseases as a punchline. What is the effect of this? How does it relate to the play's attitude towards sex more generally?
- Do Claudio and Juliet deserve to be punished? Explain your answer.
- Re-read Act 2 Scene 3. How would you describe Juliet's attitude towards her crime?
- Discuss the play's use of coin imagery, with particular attention to counterfeit coins.
- Explore the attitudes towards death presented in the play.
- Angelo's crimes are punished with marriage to Mariana. Is this a fair sentence? How would he perceive this resolution?
- When the Duke proposes marriage to Isabella, she does not give a spoken response. How do you interpret her silence?

- Robert N. Watson writes, "In *Measure for Measure* the body is in command, and the only law it respects is that of biological process" (Watson, 1994: 101). How far do you agree?

We want to hear from you!
Leave a comment on your online library
and share your favourite books on social media!

FURTHER READING

REFERENCE EDITION

- Shakespeare, W. (2008) *Measure for Measure*. London: Norton.

REFERENCE STUDIES

- British Library. (No date) Promos and Cassandra *by George Whetstone, 1578.* [Online]. [Accessed 25 November 2018]. Available from: <https://www.bl.uk/collection-items/promos-and-cassandra-by-george-whetstone-1578>

- Chedzgoy, K. (2016) *Measure for Measure*: what's the problem? *British Library.* [Online]. [Accessed 24 November 2018]. Available from: <https://www.bl.uk/shakespeare/articles/measure-for-measure-as-a-problem-play>

- McLuskie, K. E. (2016) Gender in *Measure for Measure. British Library.* [Online]. [Accessed 25 November 2018]. Available from: <https://www.bl.uk/shakespeare/articles/gender-in-measure-for-measure>

- Watson, R. N. (1994) *The Rest is Silence: Death as Annihilation in the English Renaissance.* London: University of California Press.

ADAPTATIONS

- *Measure for Measure.* (1994) [Film]. David Thacker. Dir. UK: BBC.

- *Measure for Measure.* (2006) [Film]. Bob Komar. Dir. UK: Lucky Strike Productions.

MORE FROM BRIGHTSUMMARIES.COM

- Reading guide – *Antony and Cleopatra* by William Shakespeare.

- Reading guide – *Hamlet* by William Shakespeare.

- Reading guide – *King Lear* by William Shakespeare.

- Reading guide – *Julius Caesar* by William Shakespeare.

- Reading guide – *Macbeth* by William Shakespeare.

- Reading guide – *Measure for Measure* by William Shakespeare.

- Reading guide – *The Merchant of Venice* by William Shakespeare.

- Reading guide – *A Midsummer Night's Dream* by William Shakespeare.

- Reading guide – *Much Ado About Nothing* by William Shakespeare.

- Reading guide – *Othello* by William Shakespeare.

- Reading guide – *Richard III* by William Shakespeare.

- Reading guide – *Romeo and Juliet* by William Shakespeare.

- Reading guide – *The Tempest* by William Shakespeare.

- Reading guide – *Titus Andronicus* by William Shakespeare.

- Reading guide – *Twelfth Night* by William Shakespeare.

- Reading guide – *The Two Gentlemen of Verona* by William Shakespeare.

www.brightsummaries.com

Ebook EAN: 9782808016094

Paperback EAN: 9782808016100

Legal Deposit: D/2018/12603/565

Cover: © Primento

Digital conception by Primento, the digital partner of
publishers.